SELF-ESTEEM

SEEING OURSELVES
AS GOD SEES US

JACK
KUHATSCHEK

9 STUDIES
FOR INDIVIDUALS
OR GROUPS

Life
Builder
Study

INTER-VARSITY PRESS
36 Causton Street, London SW1P 4ST, England
Email: ivp@ivpbooks.com
Website: www.ivpbooks.com

*Revised edition originally published in the United States of America in the LifeGuide® Bible
Studies series in 2002 by InterVarsity Press, Downers Grove, Illinois*
Published in Great Britain by Scripture Union in 2003
This edition published in Great Britain by Inter-Varsity Press 2018

British Library Cataloguing-in-Publication Data
A catalogue record for this book is available from the British Library.

ISBN: 978–1–78359–823–6

Printed in Great Britain by 4edge Limited, UK

*Inter-Varsity Press publishes Christian books that are true to the Bible and that communicate
the gospel, develop discipleship and strengthen the church for its mission in the world.*

*IVP originated within the Inter-Varsity Fellowship, now the Universities and Colleges Christian
Fellowship, a student movement connecting Christian Unions in universities and colleges
throughout Great Britain, and a member movement of the International Fellowship of
Evangelical Students. Website: www.uccf.org.uk. That historic association is maintained,
and all senior IVP staff and committee members subscribe to the UCCF Basis of Faith.*

Contents

Getting the Most Out of *Self-Esteem*

In Greek mythology a beautiful youth named Narcissus refused all love, including that of the mountain nymph Echo. As punishment, he was made to fall in love with his own reflection in a pool. Day after day he gazed lovingly at himself, unaware of his folly and unable to satisfy his longings.

Much of the recent emphasis on self-esteem reminds me of the story of Narcissus. People are encouraged to love themselves, to believe in themselves, to tell themselves that they are beautiful, wonderful, intelligent and capable. But as they gaze at their own reflections, they have to close one eye to the wrinkles and blemishes that also stare back at them.

The Bible does not emphasize self-love—although it does affirm our value as individuals. Scripture tells us: "Do not think of yourself more highly than you ought, but rather think of yourself with sober judgment" (Romans 12:3). What is "sober judgment"? It is a realistic appraisal of who we are—both beauty and beast, wonderful and terrible, with strengths and weaknesses. All of this should be part of our self-esteem.

The only proper mirror for seeing our true selves is God's Word. As we look in the pages of Scripture, we find much to affirm and encourage us. We discover the astonishing fact that we are God's artwork, the masterpiece of his creation. We find the answer to our longings to be loved and accepted unconditionally. Our spirits soar as we learn the wonder of what God intends us to become in Christ.

Yet Scripture also humbles us and brings us to our knees. Something is terribly wrong. The artwork has been slashed, the masterpiece defaced. Some of the beauty remains, but we are marred—the wreckage of God's original design. Only the Artist himself can begin the slow and sometimes painful process of restoration. Only he loves us enough to see the work to completion.

The biblical passages in this LifeBuilder Study can help us to see ourselves as God sees us. The first five studies provide a foundation for a healthy self-esteem. They focus on the fact that we are wonderfully made, deeply fallen, fully forgiven, eternally loved and greatly blessed.

The next four studies reveal the multifaceted and sometimes contradictory nature of every Christian. We are old yet new, weak yet strong, poor yet rich, dying yet alive.

This guide is not intended to be a resource for those seeking healing for wounded self-esteem—although those concerns are certainly valid and need to be addressed. Nor is it designed merely to help us feel better about ourselves. Rather, it is my prayer that those who use this guide will gain a biblical and balanced vision of who we are in Christ.

Suggestions for Individual Study

1. As you begin each study, pray that God will speak to you through his Word.

2. Read the introduction to the study and respond to the personal reflection question or exercise. This is designed to help you focus on God and on the theme of the study.

3. Each study deals with a particular passage—so that you can delve into the author's meaning in that context. Read and reread the passage to be studied. If you are studying a book, it will be helpful to read through the entire book prior to the first study. The questions are written using the language of the New

International Version, so you may wish to use that version of the Bible. The New Revised Standard Version is also recommended.

4. This is an inductive Bible study, designed to help you discover for yourself what Scripture is saying. The study includes three types of questions. *Observation* questions ask about the basic facts: who, what, when, where and how. *Interpretation* questions delve into the meaning of the passage. *Application* questions help you discover the implications of the text for growing in Christ. These three keys unlock the treasures of Scripture.

Write your answers to the questions in the spaces provided or in a personal journal. Writing can bring clarity and deeper understanding of yourself and of God's Word.

5. It might be good to have a Bible dictionary handy. Use it to look up any unfamiliar words, names or places.

6. Use the prayer suggestion to guide you in thanking God for what you have learned and to pray about the applications that have come to mind.

7. You may want to go on to the suggestion under "Now or Later," or you may want to use that idea for your next study.

Suggestions for Members of a Group Study

1. Come to the study prepared. Follow the suggestions for individual study mentioned above. You will find that careful preparation will greatly enrich your time spent in group discussion.

2. Be willing to participate in the discussion. The leader of your group will not be lecturing. Instead, he or she will be encouraging the members of the group to discuss what they have learned. The leader will be asking the questions that are found in this guide.

3. Stick to the topic being discussed. Your answers should be based on the verses which are the focus of the discussion and not on outside authorities such as commentaries or speakers. These studies focus on a particular passage of Scripture. Only rarely should you refer to other portions of the Bible. This allows for everyone to participate in in-depth study on equal ground.

4. Be sensitive to the other members of the group. Listen attentively when they describe what they have learned. You may be surprised by their insights! Each question assumes a variety of answers. Many questions do not have "right" answers, particularly questions that aim at meaning or application. Instead the questions push us to explore the passage more thoroughly.

When possible, link what you say to the comments of others. Also, be affirming whenever you can. This will encourage some of the more hesitant members of the group to participate.

5. Be careful not to dominate the discussion. We are sometimes so eager to express our thoughts that we leave too little opportunity for others to respond. By all means participate! But allow others to also.

6. Expect God to teach you through the passage being discussed and through the other members of the group. Pray that you will have an enjoyable and profitable time together, but also that as a result of the study you will find ways that you can take action individually and/or as a group.

7. Remember that anything said in the group is considered confidential and should not be discussed outside the group unless specific permission is given to do so.

8. If you are the group leader, you will find additional suggestions at the back of the guide.

1

Wonderfully Made

Psalm 139

A craftsman in medieval times would work for months on a special piece that displayed his finest artistic skill. Finally, when the work was finished, he would present it to the craftsmen's guild in hopes of achieving the rank of master. The work was called his masterpiece.

GROUP DISCUSSION. Describe a piece of art or other handcrafted item you really love.

What qualities must be present in a true masterpiece?

PERSONAL REFLECTION. What qualities of a masterpiece do you see in yourself?

In Psalm 139 we see God the master craftsman lovingly at work on his masterpiece. The psalm can have a profound impact on the way we view ourselves. *Read Psalm 139.*

1. How does this psalm personalize the facts that God knows everything (vv. 1-6), is present everywhere (vv. 7-12), created everything (vv. 13-18) and is perfectly holy (vv. 19-24)?

2. According to the psalmist, what specific things does the Lord know about us (vv. 1-6)?

3. How do you respond to the fact that God constantly attends to your every thought, word and action?

4. The psalmist declares that God's knowledge of him is wonderful (v. 6). Yet why do you think he feels an urge to flee from God's presence (vv. 7-12)?

5. How do you hide your true self from God?

When do you hide your true self from others?

---

6. What words are used to describe God's activity and artistry in making us (vv. 13-16)?

---

7. Do you think of yourself as God's artwork, his masterpiece? Why or why not?

---

8. David declares that God's thoughts toward us outnumber all the grains of sand (vv. 17-18). In what sense are God's constant thoughts "precious" to you?

---

9. What encouragement does this psalm offer those who view themselves as worthless?

10. How does this psalm help you to feel more loved and valued by God?

---

11. After reflecting on what he has written, why do you think the psalmist invites God to search him, know him and test him (vv. 23-24)?

Take time to thank God for the fact that you are "fearfully and wonderfully made."

Now or Later
Put verses 23-24 in your own words and express them to God in prayer.

2

Deeply Fallen

One of Michelangelo's greatest works of art, the *Pieta,* is a marble statue of Mary holding the crucified Christ. A few years ago, a madman rushed upon the statue with a sledgehammer and began defacing it. Although the damage was significant, artists were later able to restore the work to near-perfect condition.

Although we are God's artwork, we have been tragically defaced by the Fall. Yet before our restoration can begin, we must realize the extent of the damage.

GROUP DISCUSSION. What types of people do we tend to view as morally and spiritually inferior to ourselves?

PERSONAL REFLECTION. In what ways do you sense that you fall short of what God created you to be?

In Romans 3:9-20 Paul graphically describes the damage we have sustained because of sin. *Read Romans 3:9-20.*

1. Try to imagine Paul writing these verses. What do you think his mood was as he described our spiritual condition?

2. According to this passage, what is wrong with thinking we are morally and spiritually superior to others?

3. Notice the universal language in verses 10-12 ("no one," "all," "not even one"). According to Paul, what is true of everyone, without exception?

4. How do you think Paul would explain the fact that some people seem to seek after God and do good things?

5. The word *worthless* in verse 12 is also translated as "useless" (NASB) and "unprofitable" (Phillips). The word is used to describe milk that has gone sour. In what sense have we become "worthless"?

---

6. How can those who are "worthless" still have great worth to God?

---

7. In verses 13-18 Paul focuses on the various parts of our bodies—throats, tongues, lips, mouths, feet and eyes. How do these physical parts of our bodies help to describe our spiritual condition?

When all the parts are put together, what kind of portrait emerges?

8. In what ways do you see yourself in Paul's portrait?

---

9. In verses 19-20 Paul pictures a courtroom in which the prosecuting attorney reads the charges against us. What happens when it is our turn to speak and why?

---

10. In the broader context of Romans, verses 9-20 are designed to expose our need of a Savior. How do these verses highlight your need for Jesus Christ?

Why is our need for Christ a vital part of our self-esteem?

Ask God to give you a realistic picture of who you are and what you can become in Christ.

Now or Later

Pause to reflect on the following words from C. S. Lewis's classic book *Mere Christianity:* "I find I must borrow yet another parable from George MacDonald. Imagine yourself as a living house. God comes in to rebuild that house. At first, perhaps you can understand what He is doing. He is getting the drains right and stopping the leaks in the roof and so on: you knew that those jobs needed doing and so you are not surprised. But presently he starts knocking the house about in a way that hurts abominably and does not seem to make sense. What on earth is He up to? The explanation is that He is building quite a different house from the one you thought of—throwing out a new wing here, putting on an extra floor there, running up towers, making courtyards. You thought you were going to be made into a decent little cottage: but He is building a palace. He intends to come and live in it Himself" (C. S. Lewis, *Mere Christianity* [New York: MacMillan, 1952], p. 174).

3

Fully Forgiven

Hebrews 10:1-18

In a *Peanuts* cartoon, Lucy approaches Charlie Brown with a paper and pen: "Here, sign this. It absolves me of all blame." Then she goes to Schroeder: "Here, sign this. It absolves me of all blame." Finally she comes to Linus: "Here, sign this. It absolves me of all blame." As she walks away, Linus comments: "Gee, that must be a nice document to have."

GROUP DISCUSSION. What are some of the common reasons people feel guilty?

PERSONAL REFLECTION. In what ways do you struggle with a guilty conscience?

We all have various ways of dealing with our guilt. But this chapter of Hebrews describes the only true and lasting way to have a clear conscience. *Read Hebrews 10:1-18.*

1. In what ways does this passage emphasize the futility of life under the law?

In what ways do you struggle with trying to live up to your idea of "the law"?

2. Verse 1 says that the same Old Testament sacrifices were repeated endlessly year after year. What does this imply about their effectiveness (v. 2)? Explain your answer.

3. Instead of removing guilt, why did the Old Testament sacrifices sometimes produce guilt (vv. 3-4)?

4. What methods do you sometimes use to get rid of your guilt?

5. Why are our methods of atoning for our sins just as ineffective as the Old Testament sacrifices?

In light of this, why then do we sometimes feel a need for acts of self-condemnation?

6. How do Christ's sacrifice and priesthood contrast with those of the Old Testament (vv. 5-12)?

7. What specific effects does Christ's sacrifice have on us and on God (vv. 10, 14, 16-17)?

8. How does the way God views you compare with the way you view yourself?

9. Verse 18 might be paraphrased "Because God has completely forgiven you, there is nothing else you can or need to do to gain his acceptance." What effect could this have on our feelings of guilt (see v. 2)?

10. What mental or emotional barriers hinder you from viewing yourself the way God views you?

Thank God for the fact that you are fully forgiven and eternally accepted in Christ. Ask him to heighten your awareness of his grace.

Now or Later
Take time to meditate on Psalm 103:1-14. Use it as a source for prayer or journaling.

4

Eternally Loved

Romans 8:28-39

Self-esteem is sometimes built on a flimsy foundation—the way we look, how much money we make, the size of our home, even the type of car we drive. In a materialistic society our personal worth is often measured by our net worth. Judged by these standards, Jesus himself would be considered a worthless failure.

Fortunately, the world's standards are not God's standards. He does not love us because we are valuable. We are valuable because he loves us.

GROUP DISCUSSION. Why is being loved essential to our self-esteem?

PERSONAL REFLECTION. How have those who love you most affected your self-esteem?

In this passage Paul helps us grasp the breadth and depth of God's love for us. *Read Romans 8:28-39.*

1. What words would you use to describe the mood of this passage?

2. Paul speaks of "the good" and "his purpose" in verse 28. What is God's good purpose for us (v. 29)?

How might God's definition of "the good" sometimes conflict with ours?

3. In verses 29-30, five key words follow in rapid succession— *foreknew, predestined, called, justified, glorified.* How do these words provide a survey of our spiritual destiny?

4. If God is for us (vv. 31-33), what are the implications for your life?

5. Paul imagines a courtroom in which God is the judge and Jesus is our defense attorney (vv. 34-35). What charges might a prosecuting attorney bring against us?

How do God and Christ respond to these charges?

6. How might such things as trouble, hardship, famine or death (vv. 35-36) cause us to question God's love for us?

7. In what sense are we "more than conquerors" (literally, "super conquerors") over anything that threatens us (vv. 37-39)?

8. Look back over this passage. In what ways has Paul tried to convince us of God's eternal love for us?

9. How can knowing about God's love and his good purpose for us affect the way we feel about ourselves?

Thank God for his relentless and unquenchable love. Thank him for the intensity of his love, which led him to sacrifice his Son's life so that you might have life.

Now or Later

Let me no more my comfort draw
   From my frail hold of thee;
In this alone rejoice with awe—
   Thy mighty grasp of me.*

*John Stott, *The Message of Romans: God's Good News for the World* (Leicester: IVP, 1994), p. 260. Used by permission.

5

Greatly Blessed

Ephesians 1:3-14

Augustine wrote that a "Christian should be a hallelujah from head to foot." In other words, our lives should be filled with praise to God. But what if they're not? What can we do to ignite our souls when they are damp and cold?

The answer is found in Ephesians 1:3-14, which offers Paul's prescription for praise.

GROUP DISCUSSION. "Count your blessings" might sound like something your grandmother would say, but how is it also a helpful exercise?

PERSONAL REFLECTION. What blessings are you especially thankful for at this time?

Verses 3-14 are one long sentence in Greek—a sentence in which Paul overflows with praise to God. *Read Ephesians 1:3-14.*

1. Why is Paul so full of praise for God?

When have you felt like this?

2. We have been given "every spiritual blessing" in Christ (v. 3). What specific blessings are mentioned in verses 4-14?

3. How many times are the words "in Christ," "in him" or their equivalents used in verses 3-14? What is Paul trying to emphasize?

4. How should our new identity in Christ affect the way we view ourselves?

5. Verse 10 describes God's ultimate goal, not only for us but for the entire universe. How would you describe that goal in your own words?

6. To what extent do your personal goals reflect God's ultimate goal? Explain.

7. Paul uses the phrase "to the praise of his glory" three times in this passage (vv. 6, 12, 14). What does it mean to praise God's glory?

8. According to Paul, what role does praise have in our lives, both now and eternally (vv. 6, 12, 14)?

9. Praise is like a fire that needs fuel. If our lives are lacking in praise, what might Paul recommend?

Reflect on the many ways God has greatly blessed you in Christ. As you feel motivated to do so, praise God for his goodness and grace.

Now or Later

Following is Ephesians 1:3-14 in *The Message* translation by Eugene Peterson. What new insights do you learn about the blessings you have in Christ from reading this version?

> How blessed is God! And what a blessing he is! He's the Father of our Master, Jesus Christ, and takes us to the high places of blessing in him. Long before he laid down earth's foundations, he had us in mind, had settled on us as the focus of his love, to be made whole and holy by his love. Long, long ago he decided to adopt us into his family through Jesus Christ. (What pleasure he took in planning this!) He wanted us to enter into the celebration of his lavish gift-giving by the hand of his beloved Son.
>
> Because of the sacrifice of the Messiah, his blood poured out on the altar of the Cross, we're a free people—free of penalties and punishments chalked up by all our misdeeds. And not just barely free, either. *Abundantly* free! He thought of everything, provided for everything we could possibly need, letting us in on the plans he took such delight in making. He set it all out before us in Christ, a long-range plan in which everything would be brought together and summed up in him, everything in deepest heaven, everything on planet earth.
>
> It's in Christ that we find out who we are and what we are liv-

ing for. Long before we first heard of Christ and got our hopes up, he had his eye on us, had designs on us for glory living, part of the overall purpose he is working out in everything and everyone.

It's in Christ that you, once you heard the truth and believed it (this Message of your salvation), found yourselves home free—signed, sealed, and delivered by the Holy Spirit. This signet from God is the first installment on what's coming, a reminder that we'll get everything God has planned for us, a praising and glorious life.

6

Old yet New

Ephesians 4:17-32

In the movie *The Goldrush*, Charlie Chaplin is a poor prospector. In one of the opening scenes he is in a cold, rundown shack, boiling an old boot for dinner. Then he strikes it rich. As the scene changes, he is walking on the deck of a beautiful yacht, surrounded by servants and admirers. Suddenly he notices an old cigar butt that someone has discarded. Unable to resist old habits, he reaches down to pick it up. A friend intervenes, offering him a choice of fine Cuban cigars and reminding him that his old ways are no longer necessary.

GROUP DISCUSSION. Why do you think old habits are so hard to break?

PERSONAL REFLECTION. What old habits still tempt you?

In Ephesians 4 Paul urges us to lay aside our old practices as if they were worn-out clothes. He then urges us to put on the fresh new clothes we have been given in Christ. *Read Ephesians 4:17-32.*

---

1. What contrasts do you notice between "they" and "you" in this passage?

---

2. Paul insists that we no longer live like non-Christians ("Gentiles," v. 17). What is wrong with the way they think and live (vv. 17-19)?

---

3. What relationship does Paul see between a person's thoughts, character and behavior (vv. 17-19)?

---

4. Paul speaks of putting off our old self and putting on our new self (vv. 22-24). In what sense is becoming a Christian like changing clothes?

Do you see this as something we do once or as an ongoing process? Explain.

5. Our "old self" refers to our "former way of life" (v. 22). What aspects of that lifestyle does Paul urge us to put off (vv. 25-31)?

6. What "old clothes" have been the hardest for you to take off?

7. Paul says that our new self is "created to be like God" (v. 24). How is God's character reflected in the new clothes that we are to put on (vv. 25-32)?

8. How is our new self to affect our communication with others (vv. 25-32)?

our emotions and attitudes toward others?

our work?

9. Why is it important to realize that our lives are a mixture of the old and the new?

How should this awareness affect our self-esteem?

---

10. Think of one new piece of clothing you can put on today. How can it be demonstrated in your thoughts and behavior?

Like a child with a parent, ask God to help you get dressed in your new clothes.

Now or Later

In Ephesians 4:25-32 Paul gives several practical examples of the practices we should put off and put on. What are some of these practices?

How can you continue the process of "putting off" and "putting on" this week?

7

Weak yet Strong

2 Corinthians 12:1-10

Years ago the famous body builder Charles Atlas ran a magazine ad. It showed a bully kicking sand in the face of a ninety-pound weakling. The ad promised that if we followed Charles Atlas's program, we could transform our weak, puny bodies into mountains of muscle. In other words, we could kick sand in the face of the bully.

That ad captured one of the myths of our culture. We long to exchange our weaknesses for strengths, our puniness for power. Unfortunately, such myths die hard, even when we become Christians. We want to become spiritual Charles Atlases, bristling with power—all for the kingdom of God, of course.

GROUP DISCUSSION. What weakness have you longed to exchange for a strength?

PERSONAL REFLECTION. In what area do you feel like a ninety-pound weakling?

We are surprised at times when God won't cooperate by removing our weaknesses. But this passage gives us a greater shock—God prefers ninety-pound weaklings! *Read 2 Corinthians 12:1-10.*

1. What repeated words in these verses reveal Paul's primary concerns?

2. What spiritual experience does Paul "boast" about in verses 1-4?

3. Most people who boast go into great detail. Why do you think Paul is so sketchy about his experience?

4. What is the difference between boasting and a healthy sense of pride?

5. Paul was given "a thorn in [his] flesh, a messenger of Satan" (v. 7). Although we don't know the precise nature of Paul's thorn, what effect did it have on him?

6. Like Paul, we ask God to remove the "thorns" from our lives. Why does God sometimes refuse to do so?

7. Our thinking is often the opposite of God's. How can our weaknesses enhance rather than hinder our effectiveness?

8. What types of experiences would qualify as "thorns" in our lives (v. 10)?

What types of weaknesses would not qualify as thorns? Explain.

9. When have you seen God's power perfected in weakness, either in your life or someone else's?

---

10. What thorn is currently making you feel weak or humbled?

---

11. Instead of resenting and resisting that thorn, how might you "delight" in it as Paul did?

How can God's perspective on your weaknesses affect your self-esteem?

Ask God to grant you his sufficient grace—not necessarily by removing your thorn but by demonstrating his power in the midst of it.

Now or Later

To reflect on:

> Over the years I have learned that my desire to be powerful is
> really a longing for independence and self-sufficiency. After all,
> it is frustrating to be weak and dependent on someone else,
> even if the someone is God himself. . . .

> If I really got my wish for absolute strength, unlimited wealth,
> and total competence, I wouldn't feel any need for God. I would
> never experience his faithfulness or discover his sufficient
> grace. I would never learn to live in humble dependence on
> him. I would be tempted to rely on my own power instead of
> the power of God. In fact, my feelings of pride and self-suffi-
> ciency would make me believe I was a god myself.[*]

---

[*]Jack Kuhatschek, *The Superman Syndrome* (Grand Rapids, Mich.: Zondervan, 1995),
pp. 57, 59.

8

Poor yet Rich

1 Corinthians 4:8-13; 2 Corinthians 6:3-10

A few years ago a mission agency was looking for recruits. They ran an ad showing a missionary fording a river in a poor section of Africa. The man was struggling under the weight of a heavy backpack in the heat of the sun. The caption under the ad read: "In high school, John was voted the man most likely to succeed. Now look at him."

We all know that the world's standards of success are not the same as God's. Yet we often assume that God owes us a comfortable home, a secure job, decent clothes and a minimum of turmoil. When one or more of these "rights" eludes us, both our faith and our self-esteem can begin to plummet.

GROUP DISCUSSION. When hardships or difficulties enter your life, do you ever feel that God has abandoned you? Why or why not?

PERSONAL REFLECTION. How do you relate to God when you are in the midst of personal difficulties?

In these two passages in Corinthians, Paul tells us we need to readjust our thinking and our expectations. *Read 1 Corinthians 4:8-13.*

1. How would you describe Paul's mood or tone in these verses?

2. Based on Paul's description in verses 8 and 10, how do you think the Corinthians viewed themselves?

3. We normally view wealth, wisdom, honor and strength as desirable. Why then do you think Paul scolds the Corinthians?

4. How does Paul portray the life of an apostle (4:9-13)?

5. How would you feel toward God if he allowed you to be homeless, hungry, thirsty, ill-clad and brutally treated?

What would happen to your self-esteem? Explain.

6. *Read 2 Corinthians 6:3-10.* What details do these verses add to our portrait of Paul's hardships?

What do they reveal about his character?

7. In spite of his poverty and hardships, how do you think Paul was able to maintain a healthy view of God and himself (6:8-10)?

8. The Bible tells us that suffering precedes glory. In what ways are you tempted to skip over the first part, seeking glory in this present age? Explain.

9. How do your personal goals and expectations need to be revised in light of this study?

---

10. How can you have a sense of dignity and joy, regardless of your present circumstances?

Thank God for the hope we have in Christ. Ask him to help you readjust your thinking about life during this present age.

Now or Later

In Mark 8:34-35 Jesus said, "If anyone would come after me, he must deny himself and take up his cross and follow me. For whoever wants to save his life will lose it, but whoever loses his life for me and for the gospel will save it." How do his words challenge your view of life now and in the future?

9

Dying yet Alive

1 Corinthians 15:35-58

George Bernard Shaw once wrote, "The statistics on death are impressive. One out of one dies." As Christians, we must come to grips with our own mortality. Yet as we do so, we should consider something even more impressive—Christ's victory over death and his triumph over the grave.

GROUP DISCUSSION. Have you ever wished you could trade in your body now for a new, improved model? Why?

PERSONAL REFLECTION. In what ways does your mortality affect your attitude toward life?

First Corinthians 15 reveals why the tragic end of our lives is really a glorious beginning. *Read 1 Corinthians 15:35-58.*

1. In these verses Paul strains to describe the reality of the resurrection. What are some of the illustrations and examples he uses to convey this astonishing idea?

2. For obvious reasons, we view death as the end of life. According to Paul, why is it really the beginning of life (vv. 35-44)?

3. What words does Paul use to describe the bodies we now have (vv. 42-53)?

4. Do you think of your body in the terms that Paul uses? Why or why not?

5. What words does Paul use to describe our resurrection bodies (vv. 42-53)?

6. When you put all those words together, what do you imagine your resurrection body will be like?

How does it encourage you to know that you will one day be like that?

7. Why does death often feel like a crushing defeat and a poisonous sting (v. 55)?

8. How has Christ removed both the sting and victory of death (vv. 54-57)?

9. How should the knowledge of Christ's victory over death affect the way we live and work (v. 58)?

How should it affect our self-esteem?

---

10. How would you like to change how you see yourself and your life in Christ?

Like Paul (v. 57), give thanks to God who gives us the victory through our Lord Jesus Christ.

Now or Later

Book 7 of C. S. Lewis's Narnia Chronicles, *The Last Battle*, concludes with these words: "For us this is the end of all the stories, and we can most truly say that they all lived happily ever after. But for them it was only the beginning of the real story. . . . Now at last they were beginning Chapter One of the Great Story, which no one on earth has read: which goes on forever: in which every chapter is better than the one before" ([New York: Collier, 1956], p. 184). How do Lewis's words provide a fitting conclusion to this study and a hopeful perspective on our future life in Christ?

Leader's Notes

Leading a Bible discussion can be an enjoyable and rewarding experience. But it can also be *scary*—especially if you've never done it before. If this is your feeling, you're in good company. When God asked Moses to lead the Israelites out of Egypt, he replied, "O Lord, please send someone else to do it"! (Ex 4:13). It was the same with Solomon, Jeremiah and Timothy, but God helped these people in spite of their weaknesses, and he will help you as well.

You don't need to be an expert on the Bible or a trained teacher to lead a Bible discussion. The idea behind these inductive studies is that the leader guides group members to discover for themselves what the Bible has to say. This method of learning will allow group members to remember much more of what is said than a lecture would.

These studies are designed to be led easily. As a matter of fact, the flow of questions through the passage from observation to interpretation to application is so natural that you may feel that the studies lead themselves. This study guide is also flexible. You can use it with a variety of groups—student, professional, neighborhood or church groups. Each study takes forty-five to sixty minutes in a group setting.

There are some important facts to know about group dynamics and encouraging discussion. The suggestions listed below should enable you to effectively and enjoyably fulfill your role as leader.

Preparing for the Study

1. Ask God to help you understand and apply the passage in your

own life. Unless this happens, you will not be prepared to lead others. Pray too for the various members of the group. Ask God to open your hearts to the message of his Word and motivate you to action.

2. Read the introduction to the entire guide to get an overview of the entire book and the issues which will be explored.

3. As you begin each study, read and reread the assigned Bible passage to familiarize yourself with it.

4. This study guide is based on the New International Version of the Bible. It will help you and the group if you use this translation as the basis for your study and discussion.

5. Carefully work through each question in the study. Spend time in meditation and reflection as you consider how to respond.

6. Write your thoughts and responses in the space provided in the study guide. This will help you to express your understanding of the passage clearly.

7. It might help to have a Bible dictionary handy. Use it to look up any unfamiliar words, names or places. (For additional help on how to study a passage, see chapter five of *How to Lead a LifeBuilder Study*, IVP, 2018.)

8. Consider how you can apply the Scripture to your life. Remember that the group will follow your lead in responding to the studies. They will not go any deeper than you do.

9. Once you have finished your own study of the passage, familiarize yourself with the leader's notes for the study you are leading. These are designed to help you in several ways. First, they tell you the purpose the study guide author had in mind when writing the study. Take time to think through how the study questions work together to accomplish that purpose. Second, the notes provide you with additional background information or suggestions on group dynamics for various questions. This information can be useful when people have difficulty understanding or answering a question. Third, the leader's notes can alert you to potential problems you may encounter during the study.

10. If you wish to remind yourself of anything mentioned in the leader's notes, make a note to yourself below that question in the study.

Leading the Study

1. Begin the study on time. Open with prayer, asking God to help the group to understand and apply the passage.

2. Be sure that everyone in your group has a study guide. Encourage the group to prepare beforehand for each discussion by reading the introduction to the guide and by working through the questions in the study.

3. At the beginning of your first time together, explain that these studies are meant to be discussions, not lectures. Encourage the members of the group to participate. However, do not put pressure on those who may be hesitant to speak during the first few sessions. You may want to suggest the following guidelines to your group.

☐ Stick to the topic being discussed.

☐ Your responses should be based on the verses which are the focus of the discussion and not on outside authorities such as commentaries or speakers.

☐ These studies focus on a particular passage of Scripture. Only rarely should you refer to other portions of the Bible. This allows for everyone to participate in in-depth study on equal ground.

☐ Anything said in the group is considered confidential and will not be discussed outside the group unless specific permission is given to do so.

☐ We will listen attentively to each other and provide time for each person present to talk.

☐ We will pray for each other.

4. Have a group member read the introduction at the beginning of the discussion.

5. Every session begins with a group discussion question. The question or activity is meant to be used before the passage is read. The question introduces the theme of the study and encourages group members to begin to open up. Encourage as many members as possible to participate, and be ready to get the discussion going with your own response.

This section is designed to reveal where our thoughts or feelings need to be transformed by Scripture. That is why it is especially important not to read the passage before the discussion question is asked. The passage will tend to color the honest reactions people would otherwise give because they are, of course, supposed to think the way the Bible does.

You may want to supplement the group discussion question with an icebreaker to help people to get comfortable. See the community section of the *Small Group Starter Kit* (IVP, 1995) for more ideas.

You also might want to use the personal reflection question with your group. Either allow a time of silence for people to respond individually or discuss it together.

6. Have a group member (or members if the passage is long) read aloud the passage to be studied. Then give people several minutes to read the passage again silently so that they can take it all in.

7. Question 1 will generally be an overview question designed to briefly survey the passage. Encourage the group to look at the whole passage, but try to avoid getting sidetracked by questions or issues that will be addressed later in the study.

8. As you ask the questions, keep in mind that they are designed to be used just as they are written. You may simply read them aloud. Or you may prefer to express them in your own words.

There may be times when it is appropriate to deviate from the study guide. For example, a question may have already been answered. If so, move on to the next question. Or someone may raise an important question not covered in the guide. Take time to discuss it, but try to keep the group from going off on tangents.

9. Avoid answering your own questions. If necessary, repeat or rephrase them until they are clearly understood. Or point out something you read in the leader's notes to clarify the context or meaning. An eager group quickly becomes passive and silent if they think the leader will do most of the talking.

10. Don't be afraid of silence. People may need time to think about the question before formulating their answers.

11. Don't be content with just one answer. Ask, "What do the rest of you think?" or "Anything else?" until several people have given answers to the question.

12. Acknowledge all contributions. Try to be affirming whenever possible. Never reject an answer. If it is clearly off-base, ask, "Which verse led you to that conclusion?" or again, "What do the rest of you think?"

13. Don't expect every answer to be addressed to you, even though this will probably happen at first. As group members become more at ease, they will begin to truly interact with each other. This is one sign of healthy discussion.

14. Don't be afraid of controversy. It can be very stimulating. If you don't resolve an issue completely, don't be frustrated. Move on and keep it in mind for later. A subsequent study may solve the problem.

15. Periodically summarize what the group has said about the passage. This helps to draw together the various ideas mentioned and gives continuity to the study. But don't preach.

16. At the end of the Bible discussion you may want to allow group members a time of quiet to work on an idea under "Now or Later." Then discuss what you experienced. Or you may want to encourage group members to work on these ideas between meetings. Give an opportunity during the session for people to talk about what they are learning.

17. Conclude your time together with conversational prayer, adapting the prayer suggestion at the end of the study to your group. Ask for God's help in following through on the commitments you've made.

18. End on time.

Many more suggestions and helps are found in *How to Lead a LifeBuilder Study*.

Components of Small Groups

A healthy small group should do more than study the Bible. There are four components to consider as you structure your time together.

Nurture. Small groups help us to grow in our knowledge and love of God. Bible study is the key to making this happen and is the foundation of your small group.

Community. Small groups are a great place to develop deep friendships with other Christians. Allow time for informal interaction before and after each study. Plan activities and games that will help you get to know each other. Spend time having fun together—going on a picnic or cooking dinner together.

Worship and prayer. Your study will be enhanced by spending time praising God together in prayer or song. Pray for each other's needs—and keep track of how God is answering prayer in your group. Ask God to help you to apply what you are learning in your study.

Outreach. Reaching out to others can be a practical way of applying what you are learning, and it will keep your group from becoming self-focused. Host a series of evangelistic discussions for your friends or neighbors. Clean up the yard of an elderly friend. Serve at a soup kitchen together, or spend a day working in the community.

Many more suggestions and helps in each of these areas are found in the *Small Group Starter Kit*. You will also find information on building a small group. Reading through the starter kit will be worth your time.

Study 1. Wonderfully Made. Psalm 139.

Purpose: To see ourselves as God's creative masterpiece.

Question 1. The psalm is actually a prayer to God to examine our hearts, but it also reveals the Lord's activity in creating and caring for us.

Question 3. Some members of the group may find such attention comforting and encouraging. Others may find it intimidating. Allow people to be honest with their responses.

Question 4. Derek Kidner writes: "The impulse to flee from God's face (the literal meaning of *thy presence*) is as old as the Fall. Admittedly the talk of flight may be a purely literary device to dramatize the fact of God's ubiquity; but there seems to be at least an ambivalent attitude to him here, like that of a child running from its parent. . . . Amos 9:2ff. uses imagery that recalls this very passage to describe the hunting down of those who are fugitives from justice. If no thought of escape had come to mind here, David could have cried 'What shall separate me from thy Spirit, or drive me from thy presence?', somewhat as Paul did in Romans 8:38ff. But the end of the psalm will see no doubts or hesitations" (*Psalms 73—150,* Tyndale Old Testament Commentaries, ed. D. J. Wiseman [Nottingham: IVP,

2014], pp. 500–501).

Question 6. *Created* (literally, "brought forth"), *knit, woven*—the words suggest God's attention to every detail of our being. The latter two words suggest "the complex patterns and colours of the weaver or embroiderer" (Kidner, *Psalms*, p. 466).

Questions 7 & 9. The challenge of this or any other portion of Scripture is to see ourselves as God sees us. Many Christians have been taught to view themselves as worthless junk. Although God's creative masterpiece has been defaced by the Fall, much of the original beauty remains. Encourage your group to focus on that beauty.

Question 8. God's infinite thoughts toward us are evidence that he greatly values what he creates. He is lovingly interested in every detail of our lives.

Question 11. The psalm begins and ends with God's searching activity. The psalmist realizes that the God who lovingly and carefully made him, and who attends to his every thought and action, can be trusted to gently bring to light those areas that need his healing touch.

Study 2. Deeply Fallen. Romans 3:9-20.

Purpose: To grasp the extent of our fallen condition so that we can allow God to begin the process of restoring us to his image.

Question 1. Clearly Paul was angry. Picture him stomping around and fuming, then grabbing his pen and parchment to write a terse note. Maybe someone in the group would like to dramatize it.

Question 2. Verses 9-20 are the culmination of Paul's opening argument in chapters 1—3. In chapter 1 he charged that the Gentiles are guilty. In chapter 2 he charged that the Jews are also guilty. Now he merely restates what he has already demonstrated—that the whole world justly deserves God's condemnation because of sin.

Question 3. Paul is merely echoing the verdict of Scripture by quoting from several Old Testament passages: Psalms 14:1-3; 53:1-3; Ecclesiastes 7:20; Psalms 5:9; 140:3; Isaiah 59:7-8; Psalm 36:1.

Question 4. The answer to this question cannot be found in the text, but it is important to wrestle with it anyway. Paul's portrait is so stark that it seems to conflict with our experience.

It is helpful to remember that throughout Romans 1:1—3:20 Paul's argument is directed to those outside of Christ. In other New Testament passages we discover that if a person truly seeks after God, it is only because the grace of God has been active in his or her life. Apart from God's grace, our sinful tendency is to reject and run from him.

Questions 5-6. We are worthless in the eyes of the law (because we cannot keep it), not in the eyes of God. Some members of the group may use verses like these to confirm their feelings of worthlessness. However, although we are sinful, fallen and complete failures in the eyes of the law, we are still of great value to God. Otherwise, he would not have sent his only Son to die for us.

In answering question 6, it might be helpful to refer the group back to Psalm 139, which was the focus of the previous study.

Question 7. In a graphic way Paul describes what has been called our "total depravity." Although we are not necessarily as bad as we could be, every aspect of our being has been affected by sin.

Question 9. If time permits, you may also want to ask: "How do history and current events confirm the accuracy of Paul's portrait?" To enhance the discussion, you may wish to bring clippings from current newspapers and magazines.

Study 3. Fully Forgiven. Hebrews 10:1-18.

Purpose: To realize that because of Christ there is nothing more we can or need to do about our sin.

Question 2. It is clear that the sacrifices were ineffective. However, the author of Hebrews goes beyond this fact to explain how he knows they were ineffective. Encourage your group to briefly discuss his explanation.

Question 3. The author of Hebrews points out the irony that the very sacrifices that were supposed to remove guilt actually reminded the people each year that their guilt remained. Why did it remain? Because the sacrifices were totally unable to do what only Christ could do: take away the sins and guilt of the people.

Question 5. The unending, ineffective and guilt-producing sacrifices of the Old Testament are like a parable of our own methods of dealing with our sins. Instead of relying totally on the once-for-all sacrifice of

Christ, we sometimes feel a need for acts of penance or self-condemnation. We may feel that such acts help to appease an angry God, but they are merely an insult to the sufficiency of Christ's death.
Question 6. They offered sacrifices and burnt offerings; Jesus offered himself. The priests performed the same duties again and again; Jesus performed his only once. The priests constantly stood while performing their duties—a sign of unfinished work; Christ sat down after completing his work for all eternity.
Questions 7-8. We have been "made holy" (v. 10), we have been made "perfect forever" (v. 14), and we are in the process of having God's law written on our hearts and minds by his Spirit (v. 16). In addition, the Lord himself states that "their sins and lawless acts I will remember no more."

The author of Hebrews could not state more strongly the completely effective work of Christ on our behalf. We may view ourselves as sinful, but God views us as holy in Christ. We may grieve over our imperfections, but God views us as perfect in Christ. We may constantly feel guilty over our sins, but God has forgiven and forgotten them in Christ! Instead of focusing on ourselves, we should focus on our Savior.
Question 9. Only those who have an accurate view of Christ and his work can have an accurate view of themselves. If we think too little of ourselves, it may be that we think too little of Christ.

Study 4. Eternally Loved. Romans 8:28-39.
Purpose: To begin to grasp the depth of God's eternal love for us.
Question 2. Romans 8:28 is often quoted as a promise that nothing bad will happen to us as Christians. Unfortunately, that is not the case. We are as susceptible to evil and misfortune as anyone. Yet no matter what happens to us, God uses the events of our lives to bring about our highest good—conformity to the image of his Son.
Question 3. *Foreknew:* God knew beforehand—even before the creation of the world (see Eph 1:4)—who would believe in Christ. *Predestined*: He guides the lives of those he foreknew so that they will achieve their destiny. *Called:* At the proper time he calls them to faith in Christ, and they respond as he knew they would and as he destined

them to respond. *Justified*: At the moment of faith they are justified, legally declared righteous before God. *Glorified*: Ultimately, they will be glorified, completely transformed by the Spirit to the image of Christ—an event so certain to occur that Paul speaks of it in the past tense. From beginning to end God guides and directs our lives toward that good purpose he has planned for us in his Son.

Question 4. Paul argues from the greater to the lesser. If God did not withhold the greatest gift from us—his only Son—why would he withhold any lesser gifts?

Question 5. Although the prosecuting attorney might bring many true charges against us, he does not stand a chance of winning the case. Why? Because God himself, who is the ultimate judge, has already declared us righteous in Christ. And because Jesus himself, our defense attorney, not only died for us but now constantly intercedes for us. His resurrection and position of highest honor at God's right hand proves that his sacrifice for us was accepted. Therefore, we are completely acquitted and fully acceptable to God in Christ.

Question 6. The biblical pattern is that the suffering of this present age precedes the glory of the age to come (see Rom 8:17). For those who expect glory now, such things as trouble, hardship, famine or death come as a shock, and they wonder whether God has failed them and whether he truly loves them. The fault is not with God's love or faithfulness but with their faulty perspective.

Question 7. How can a dead person be considered victorious? Only if his ultimate victory comes not in this life but at the resurrection, when all of God's loving purposes for us will be completely fulfilled.

Study 5. Greatly Blessed. Ephesians 1:3-14.

Purpose: To realize that we have been blessed with every spiritual blessing in Christ.

Question 2. Paul states that our blessings are "in the heavenly realms" (v. 3). This phrase occurs five times in Ephesians and refers to the realm where Christ is seated at the right hand of God, the place of highest honor and blessing. Because we are "in Christ," we partake of the blessings bestowed on him. The word *redemption* (v. 7) may be unfamiliar to some in the group. The term is borrowed from the slave market. A person would pay a price to buy someone out of slavery. In a similar fashion, Christ paid the price of his own death in order to free us from our slavery to sin and death.

Question 5. Here's what the *NIV Study Bible* has to say about verse 10: 'To bring . . . under one head.' Paul uses a significant term here that not only has the idea of leadership but also was often used of adding up a column of figures. A contemporary way of putting it might be to say that in a world of confusion, where things do not 'add up' or make sense, we look forward to the time when everything will be brought into meaningful relationship under the headship of Christ" ([Grand Rapids, Mich.: Zondervan, 1985], p. 1793).

Questions 7-8. Although God's glory is often portrayed as a brilliant light (Ps 104:2) or a bright cloud (1 Kings 8:10-11), such things merely symbolize the brilliance of God's character and the brightness of his love and grace. We will spend eternity praising God for who he is and what he has done for us in Christ (Eph 1:12).

Question 9. If our lives are lacking in praise, Paul would recommend that we take a fresh look at all that God has done for us in Christ. The first three chapters of Ephesians would be a good place to begin. For a longer look, consider the first eight chapters of Romans.

Study 6. Old yet New. Ephesians 4:17-32.

Purpose: To consider that even though we are new in Christ, we must still lay aside old habits and practices.

Question 2. The Gentiles of Paul's day represented those outside of Israel and therefore outside of a covenant relationship with God. Although Paul's description is two thousand years old, it sounds very contemporary: "Having lost all sensitivity, they have given themselves over to sensuality so as to indulge in every kind of impurity, with a continual lust for more" (v. 19).

Question 3. Notice the progression from *thoughts* ("darkened in their understanding") to *inner character* ("the hardening of their hearts") to *behavior* ("they have given themselves over to . . ."). However the progression is not necessarily in a straight line, since the Gentiles' ignorance in verse 18 is attributed to their hardness of heart. Obviously, there is a continual interplay among our thoughts, our character and our behavior, with each one affecting the other.

Questions 4-5. Colossians 3:9-10 states that we have already put off our old self and put on our new self, presumably at conversion. He writes: "Do not lie to each other, since you have taken off your old self with its practices and have put on the new self, which is being renewed in knowledge in the image of its Creator." Even in Ephesians, Paul's instructions to "put off" and "put on" are related to what he "taught" (past tense) the Ephesians from the beginning. Nevertheless, both in Ephesians and in Colossians Paul sees no contradiction between commanding his readers to *be* what they have *already become* in Christ, or to act in harmony with their new standing in Christ.

By using the image of putting on new clothes, Paul may be alluding to the fact that baptismal candidates changed into white robes (A. Skevington Wood, *Ephesians*, The Expositor's Bible Commentary [Grand Rapids, Mich.: Zondervan, 1978], p. 62).

Question 7. Although Paul is describing our character rather than God's, it is a helpful exercise to think about how God's character is reflected in the qualities Paul mentions. One explicit example is seen in verse 32, where we are urged to forgive others because God has forgiven us in Christ.

Question 9. The Christian life is often described as a before-and-after story, in which everything since our conversion is all happy and harmonious. Some even go so far as to claim that they live in complete freedom from all known sin. To do so, however, such people must either lower their standards of holiness or else live in self-delusion.

Others go to an opposite extreme. They are overwhelmed by the sin which remains in their lives and conclude that they are hopeless failures as Christians.

We need to have a more balanced perspective. From the moment we become Christians until the time Christ returns, we live in a tension between the old and the new, between the already and the not-yet. We are new people in Christ, and there are many evidences of that newness in the ways we think and live. Yet we still struggle with many of our old thoughts and patterns of behavior. Both sides of the tension are true; both must be acknowledged if we are to have a healthy self-esteem.

Study 7. Weak yet Strong. 2 Corinthians 12:1-10.
Purpose: To realize that God's power is best seen not by him removing our weaknesses but by giving us grace in the midst of our weaknesses.
Question 2. Paul describes "a man" who was caught up to the "third heaven," the realm beyond the first heaven of our earth's atmosphere and beyond the second heaven of outer space. The third heaven is the dwelling place of God.
Question 3. Because Paul describes his experiences in the third person ("he heard" rather than "I heard"), some have concluded that he is not speaking about himself. However, it is much more likely that Paul is deliberately distancing himself from these experiences because he is uncomfortable about having to boast. Verse 7 makes it clear that those remarkable experiences are his own.
Question 4. Healthy pride is based on reality, while false pride is often distorted and shame-based. According to Paul, he could have legitimately boasted about his spiritual experiences because they really happened. Yet he chose not to boast because he wanted people's opinion of him to be based on his actions and words rather than his credentials (v. 6).
Question 5. For centuries people have speculated about the precise nature of Paul's thorn. They have suggested that it was headaches or earaches, eye disease or malarial fever. Others have claimed it was epilepsy or a speech impediment, hypochondria, deafness or remorse for persecuting Christians. Still others have suggested gallstones, gout, rheumatism, a dental infection—even lice! Whatever it was, the thorn humbled Paul, making him feel weak and dependent on God.
Question 8. Paul gives us several examples in verse 10: weaknesses, insults, hardships, persecutions and difficulties of various types. Obviously our sins would not qualify as the kind of thorn that God would choose not to remove.

Study 8. Poor yet Rich. 1 Corinthians 4:8-13; 2 Corinthians 6:3-10.
Purpose: To grasp the fact that we are rich in Christ regardless of how much money or power or prestige we have in this present age.
Question 3. Paul does not scold the Corinthians because they have

these things but because they assume that they are rich and glorious when in fact they are spiritually immature and boastful.

Questions 4-5. Many of us would feel completely abandoned by God if he allowed such things to happen to us. Such hardships would cause us to question God's goodness and love.

The truth is that God has repeatedly told us that we will experience suffering in this present age (Jn 16:33; Rom 8:17-25; 2 Cor 4:7-15). Perhaps the problem is that many evangelicals have wedded Christianity and the American dream. We assume that God owes us a good-paying job, an upwardly mobile career, a loving spouse, two or three children, a house in the suburbs and a trouble-free life. Instead of questioning God's goodness when our dreams fail to materialize, what we need is to rethink our view of life during this present age. We also need to realize the true wealth we do possess in Christ.

Question 7. Paul knows that what is visible to the world—his poverty and suffering—does not reveal the full reality of his life. Even though he is unknown by the world, he is known and loved by God. Even though he is sorrowful because of his sufferings, he has many reasons to rejoice in Christ. Even though he is poor by the world's standards, he possesses untold riches in Christ. Even though his ministry exposes him to a living death, he possesses eternal life and the promise of resurrection. His healthy view of God and himself resulted from seeing the unseen through the eyes of faith.

Study 9. Dying yet Alive. 1 Corinthians 15:35-58.
Purpose: To grasp the fact that the seemingly tragic end of our lives is really a glorious beginning.

Question 4. Paul mentions that our resurrection body will be a "spiritual body" (v. 44). *Spiritual* does not mean nonmaterial but rather "from heaven" as opposed to "of the dust of the earth" (v. 47). Christ's own resurrection demonstrates that our bodies will be physical (see Lk 24:36-39), although they will also be changed—prepared for life in the kingdom of God.

Questions 7-8. "The sting of death is sin, and the power of sin is the law" (v. 56): Sin brings the sting of death because death is the penalty for sin. The law gives sin its power because the law reveals our sin and condemns it, demanding our death.

Christ has removed the sting of death because those who belong to him immediately pass into his presence (Lk 23:42-43; 2 Cor 5:1-10; Phil 1:19-26). Christ has removed the victory of the grave because all who believe in him will be raised from the dead.

Question 9. Our own mortality reminds us that this present life is fragile and temporary. Because this present age is quickly passing away, we should follow Paul's example: "So we fix our eyes not on what is seen, but on what is unseen. For what is seen is temporary, but what is unseen is eternal" (2 Cor 4:18). Only those who view their mortality in light of the resurrection can have a proper view of themselves and a proper view of their place in the world.

Question 10. If time permits, you may want to ask a review question before closing in prayer. For example, you might ask: "How has the way God views you affected the way you view yourself?" Or "What have you enjoyed most about this series on self-esteem?"

Jack Kuhatschek was formerly an executive vice president and publisher at Baker Publishing Group. He is the author of many Bible study guides including Romans *and* David *in the LifeBuilder Bible Study series, and the books* Applying the Bible *and* The Superman Syndrome.